CAREER AS A

LAWYER

GENERAL PRACTICE ATTORNEY

"YOU'VE BEEN SERVED!" THOSE ARE SCARY WORDS.
Nobody likes to get legal documents. They are confusing,
intimidating, and most people have no idea what to
make of them. Unless, of course, you are a lawyer. When

it comes to legal matters, most of us are at a loss without the guidance of a knowledgeable lawyer. Attorneys help us understand our complicated legal system. They make sense out of all those wherefores and whereases ordinary people cannot decipher.

General practice attorneys handle a wide variety of legal matters, shifting gears from one area of the law to another throughout the day to assist their clients. They use their expertise to guide people through a complex maze of laws, explaining in plain English exactly what is going on. Then they turn their attention to what needs to be done to resolve the problem.

General practice attorneys are equally at ease reading through a lengthy, multifaceted contract and suggesting revisions that benefit their client, and appearing in municipal court to defend someone charged with a series of traffic violations. A general practitioner serves as a confidant, an advisor in a time of crisis, a voice of reason when emotions may cloud a client's judgment, a defender, an advocate, and, many times, a friend when one is hard to find.

While the ranks of lawyers have swelled over the years, so has the need for attorneys, as modern-day society has grown more complex. Who would have thought a decade or so ago that the skills of an attorney might be needed to battle a variety of violations brought on by the use of computers, from identity theft to fraud to invasion of privacy to cyberbullying?

Some might say general practice lawyers handle all the cases nobody else wants. Yet that makes those cases that much more important. Who else will stand up for these individuals and aid them in their time of need?

This is not a job for the faint-hearted. There will be many

times during your career as a lawyer in general practice that you will have to counsel people about some difficult, life-altering decisions they will have to make. General practice attorneys give their clients the peace of mind that someone is willing to speak on their behalf and tell their side of the story. These professionals protect their clients' property, their rights, and their good name, and make sure they are not overlooked in the often uncaring, baffling, and impersonal judicial system.

WHAT YOU CAN DO NOW

YOU PROBABLY HAVE MOST OF YOUR IMPRESSIONS of the legal profession from the way attorneys are portrayed on television. The reality is quite a bit different.

This job calls for endless hours of reading, research, and writing, which rarely makes it into action-packed TV scripts. Depending on the cases you get, you are not likely to see much courtroom drama as a lawyer in general practice.

Not everyone is cut out to be an attorney, so you should do some research before planning a legal career. Many lawyers would be happy to have you come into the office for a while and shadow them. That way you can see firsthand what the job entails. You will not be able to sit in on private conferences, but you probably will get a chance to read some briefs, motions, and court transcripts, and see if you find the work intriguing. Ask the lawyer you are shadowing questions about the career. That is the best way to learn what the job is about.

If there is a municipal court near you, take the time to go down to observe hearings and trials, which are usually open to the public, and watch the judicial system in action.

HISTORY OF THE CAREER

IN ANCIENT ATHENS, GREECE, A CITY with a vibrant legal system, citizens used to bring complaints they had against other citizens to a court, where a jury of citizens would decide the case. In hopes of persuading the jury to see the case their way, citizens would hire orators, people with polished public speaking skills, to present their case. Many of these orators were familiar with court procedure and the law, and could cleverly craft a person's case to sway the jury. These orators could be considered the first lawyers.

The legal system in ancient Athens bore many similarities to the one we are familiar with today in the United States. However, it was Britain's King Henry II in 1154 who established *common law,* a unified code of laws that applied throughout the nation. That legal system ended the use of random remedies, and provided uniformity in the British judicial system. The legal system instituted by King Henry II is the one American colonists brought with them to the New World.

Changes occurred through the years, among them the more dominant role attorneys started to play toward the end of the 17th century, as laws became more complicated. Anyone in the American colonies who wanted to be a lawyer went to England to study the law, and then returned to the colonies to go into practice. Lawyers played a key role in colonial America, especially as intercolonial and transatlantic trade grew and disputes over that trade became commonplace.

Delaware was the first colony to require people to prove themselves worthy of practicing the law. Starting in 1763, anyone who wanted to be a lawyer in Delaware had to pass an oral examination administered by a judge. Other colonies quickly followed suit. After passing the exam, prospective attorneys were admitted to an association of lawyers in their colony, known as the bar. The term *bar* came from a 16th-century English custom of having law students admitted to a professional legal association, known as the Inns of the Court, before practicing law. Before they could join the association, students had to undergo rigorous questioning about the law by benchers, who were senior members of the Inns of the Court. The students would sit on one side of the room where the questioning took place; the benchers sat on the other side. A wooden bar, like a bannister, in the middle of the room, separated them. Following the questioning, students whom the benchers felt knew enough about the law were told to step around the bar and join the profession; hence the term "passing the bar."

Lawyers figured prominently in the founding of this country. Thomas Jefferson, Alexander Hamilton, John Jay, John Marshall, John Adams, and Patrick Henry were all attorneys. Of the 56 men who signed the Declaration of Independence in 1776, 25 were lawyers. Of the 55 delegates who attended the Constitutional Convention in 1787, 34 were attorneys. Over half of those lawyers were veterans of the Revolutionary War, and they had a clear vision of the laws that were needed to govern the new nation.

Following the War of Independence, an excellent teacher

of law, Connecticut attorney Tapping Reeve founded the Litchfield Law School in 1784. The school attracted students from all over the new nation. In 1799, the College of William and Mary in Virginia made George Wythe the nation's first law professor on the university level. Thomas Jefferson had served as an apprentice under Wythe. The modern law school started to take shape in 1817, when Harvard University opened its law school in Cambridge, the oldest continually operating law school in the nation.

Initially, women were denied entry to law school, and if they studied the law on their own, they were banned from being admitted to the bar. Belle Babb Mansfield was the first woman to be admitted to a state bar in the nation. In 1869, the Iowa state bar admitted Mansfield after she challenged the rule, in the Iowa state courts, barring women from practicing law. She won the case, which proved she was a good attorney! Women fought and won admission to bars in other states as well, although women would not take their rightful place in the ranks of attorneys for another century.

Life in the United States became more complicated in the 20th century. Many new laws were being passed, dealing with everything from business practices to inheritance. By the mid-1950s, many lawyers felt the legal field was expanding too rapidly for them to be experts in every aspect of the law. That prompted the era of specialization. There were many attorneys, however, who felt they could better serve their clients by being well versed in as much of the law as possible, and they embraced general practice law. Many young attorneys today, looking for a practice that offers variety and a wide range of cases, find the idea of a general law practice highly appealing.

WHERE YOU WILL WORK

LAWYERS ARE NEEDED EVERYWHERE, so there are no geographic restrictions on where a lawyer works. You do not have to travel to one area of the country or another because it is the hub of legal activity. People need attorneys as much in rural and suburban areas as they do in large cities. You will find big law firms in business parks in suburbia as well as in skyscrapers in the nation's most populous cities. Sole practitioners work in the heart of rural America as well as in storefronts in the country's largest cities.

We are a nation of laws, and people everywhere need legal counsel. If you want to be a country lawyer in the small town where you grew up, you can certainly make a good living. You can also battle the crowds on Wall Street in New York City and work in one of the busy offices in that bustling downtown neighborhood.

Attorneys in general practice are not limited to being in their own practice or in a firm. Many companies have their own in-house legal departments with lawyers employed on staff to handle legal matters from contracts, to lawsuits filed against the corporation. These companies may have a single lawyer or an entire team.

The government also employs lawyers. All branches of government need lawyers, and while some of these lawyers specialize in specific areas, like criminal matters or environmental law, many serve as general counsel to municipalities, county and state governments, and the federal government as well.

Small towns often employ a lawyer who serves in a

part-time capacity as municipal attorney. That person may also be able to maintain a private general practice as long as none of the work is in conflict with matters the lawyer is handling on behalf of the town.

Nonprofits have attorneys working for them. Some of this work is done on an as-needed basis, but the large nonprofits have lawyers on staff to handle issues that come up on a daily basis. Educational institutions, like colleges and universities, employ lawyers.

Being in general practice lends itself well to having your office in your home. This allows you to keep your costs and fees down, making you more competitive in the marketplace.

THE WORK YOU WILL DO

ASK ANYONE WHO HAS FARED WELL in a legal matter why it worked out the way it did and the answer is usually: "I had a good lawyer." The work you do for your clients can affect them for the rest of their lives. That is especially true for lawyers in general practice because of the wide range of work you do for a client throughout an entire lifetime. This may include real estate closings, tax issues, wills and estates, bankruptcy, foreclosure, matrimonial issues, immigration, adoption, traffic violations, setting up a business, trusts, workers' compensation, and debt disputes, among many other issues.

You start with information gathering. Lawyers cannot possibly evaluate a case and the work that needs to be done without having all the facts, or as many of them as possible. For example, if you are writing a will for a person, you need to know exactly all the details about the clients possessions and heirs. The same is true with a contract or any other legal document you are writing specifically for your client.

Other cases are more complicated, like criminal matters, personal injury, landlord-tenant disputes, divorce, and child custody. For these types of cases, some of the information you need can be obtained directly from the client. Other details you have to uncover from a variety of sources, including police reports, witnesses, your client's friends and relatives, doctors' reports, insurance documents, evidence that has been collected in connection with the case, court documents and other resources.

It is always best to talk to as many people as possible. Good lawyers possess top-notch interviewing skills and the ability to elicit information. To get substantive answers, you have to ask probing questions. When you are interviewing anyone involved in a case, you have to know the case and the subject matter well enough to craft pertinent questions. In getting answers to those questions, you come up with the information you are looking for to help build or defend your case. Part of your preparation might involve going to the scene of an incident, to see it for yourself. Things look different in person, and that can have an impact on your perspective on the case.

While you are assembling the specifics, you can begin developing the strategy you are going to use in the case. Your plan of attack may change as you get further into a case, but it is good to have an initial game plan to follow as the pieces of the case start to come together. You determine who you think is right and who is wrong. Is somebody lying or just confused? In the conflicting information, can you find a way to prove your client's version of the story, or are you going to have to dig a bit deeper to prove that your client's adversary in the case is being deceitful? Sometimes a case comes down to much more than who is right and who is wrong. It is a matter of what the law is and what the law means.

No lawyer is familiar with every law or every precedent. To win your case, you will spend a great deal of time doing legal research. As you examine each precedent-setting case you hope will shed light on the matter you are investigating, you are learning things that could help in another case you are working on now or in the future. Done behind the scenes, research is often underappreciated, but wins the day in the long run. Research is required in nearly all aspects of legal work, not just preparation for a case going to court. Writing motions and briefs depends on quality research. Some of the simplest questions about a will or a contract may send you to the law books to check a minor detail to make sure the document you write cannot be challenged later on.

Some of your time will be spent deciding what is the best way to represent your client. In municipal court, for instance, is it better for your client to plead guilty to a reduced charge, if you can arrange for a lesser punishment, or to take his chances before a municipal court judge? The client may feel he has a strong case, but there are few winners in municipal court, other than the town, which makes money from fines and court costs. You may have to advise your client to take the plea.

Lawyers in general practice do appear in court, but most lawyers try to do everything they can do to avoid going to court. In court, anything can happen. As a result, lawyers generally try to settle cases. Personal injury, divorce, child custody, landlord-tenant, creditor disputes, and many other matters, even criminal charges, can be settled out of court, sparing the client the expense and stress, and uncertainty of a court appearance.

Negotiating settlements will probably be one of the toughest aspects of your job, but one of the most satisfying as well. Court cases often end in an all-or-nothing outcome. There is a clear winner and a clear loser, but both sides often sustain a heavy toll emotionally. By contrast, in a settlement, both sides have a chance of walking away with some partial victory, even if it is just not having to pay as much in damages as the client feared. These settlements do not come about easily. It could take months, if not years, to work out a settlement. You could arrange a settlement and bring it back to your client, who then rejects it, and sends you back to the negotiating table. Settlement talks may break down numerous times. Sometimes settlement talks take place over the telephone. Other times you are spending hours in a settlement conference, striving to forge a compromise.

Sometimes your client is as stubborn as the opposition, and there is no justifiable reason for the dispute to go on. You will have to talk some sense into your client, and the opposing counsel will have to do the same on the other side. A settlement can be reached, only to be stalled as differences arise in the details. Perseverance and patience are required to get the job done and you will need plenty of both.

If a case does go to court, you will spend weeks preparing for trial. It will not be your only case. You will need to budget your time wisely so you can prepare your case for court but not overlook your other clients, especially if an emergency comes up.

Before you go to court, you have to prepare your witnesses. Anybody you call to the witness stand to give testimony on behalf of your client has to be prepped about what to say while on the stand and how to respond to what might be asked by opposing counsel.

After the trial, there might be appeals, and not only if you lose in a criminal case. Most civil cases can be appealed as well. Lawyers take care of filing all the paperwork involved in the appeals process.

When you are in general practice law, you cannot minimize your role as an advisor. Life is complicated, and people will seek out your insight in hopes of staving off legal problems. At times, things can be resolved with a simple letter or a phone call. Sometimes it requires more action. Some of the more common questions you get will come from people who own or want to start their own businesses. A lawyer's input will give prospective business owners the information they need to set up the business properly in a way best suited for them and the industry they are in. Part of your job will be to take care of the myriad legal issues involved in establishing that business. For those who are already in business, there are always disputes, and your views may help settle the matter quickly before it gets blown out of proportion.

As an advisor, you are also a voice of reason. "I'll sue" is always the battle cry, but not necessarily the prudent course of action. Lawyers are supposed to find solutions in everyone's best interest, if that is at all possible.

Keep in mind that, as an attorney, you are running a business as a sole proprietor or in a partnership. You will have to spend some of your time managing the business. You might have an office manager, but you still have to stay on top of things to make sure the business is being run properly, and making a profit. If any problems come up, you will have to handle them.

You will also find that you have a role as a consultant to other attorneys, and you might someday seek out their advice on a case you are handling. The law can be baffling and sometimes talking a case out with another lawyer makes things clearer.

LAWYERS TELL THEIR OWN STORIES

I Am a Sole Practitioner

"I am a sole practitioner, but I am far from alone. While I am the only lawyer in the office, I have two full-time paralegals, a part-time legal assistant, a legal secretary, and a regular secretary. I also have a private detective who does freelance investigative work for me when it's needed.

I have a general law practice and handle all kinds of cases, from criminal to matrimonial to estates. I have been a sole practitioner for 25 years and wouldn't have it any other way. I went to law school because I wanted to help people. I never wanted to lose that desire because I felt that it gave me an edge in this profession. I represent clients because I feel the case has merit and I can make a difference. You can't win them all, but you can try, and when you don't win, maybe you are able to help in some way.

In my practice I don't look at clients as my income; I look at them as people. There are no senior partners breathing down my neck, pushing me to rack up billable hours to pay high salaries. I can give clients and cases the time they deserve. I give my clients all types of ways to contact me – including mail, phone, email, fax – and I want to hear from them. I like that I am able to establish a one-on-one relationship with my clients. They don't get lost in a maze of fancy offices and uncaring associates.

For me, there could be nothing worse than some senior partner telling me I have put too much time into a case and I should find some way to get rid of it. I think that's shameful. That's not why I got into this field. As a sole practitioner, I can go the extra mile, put in some additional time on a case, simply because I want to and feel it's the right thing to do. I have a great deal of independence.

I shoulder a lot of responsibility, but that would be the same in just about any business. Sole practitioners have to budget their time wisely and not overextend themselves. They have to assemble a team that makes their job easier. They have to know how to work smart. They reap the rewards when a client sees everything work out all right and realizes there is justice."

I Am an Attorney in a Small Law Firm

"We have three lawyers in our firm, and this is exactly the type of work environment I like. I enjoy the independence of being in a small law firm. Each of us seeks out and brings in clients, and some clients simply walk in the door.

Our office is located in a suburb, but we are close enough to an urban area to bring in clients from the neighboring city. We are all involved in civic organizations, and we often get clients from the people we meet through our volunteer efforts at a Rotary Club, the Chamber of Commerce, or even coaching the Little League. Our biggest advertising is word of mouth. A happy client refers another client. We have clients who have been with us for years.

We provide a variety of services to our clients because we have a general practice. Usually we handle the legal matters of an entire family. I think it is the variety that drew me to a general practice. Each partner has a comfort zone, the cases we like handling the most. I like to take cases every once in a while that are a stretch. It is one of the ways you grow as an attorney. I am successful with those cases, though they might be a bit tougher, like a case involving harassment in the workplace.

Having other lawyers in the office is nice because you can run ideas by them and have them look at a case with a fresh pair of eyes. If you need someone to fill in for you, someone is sitting in the next office. The difference between our small firm and a law office with tens if not hundreds of lawyers is that the three of us come at cases from the same philosophy. No one's case is more important than another's. We give every client the same attention and the same effort.

I was never one for the luxurious office. It doesn't make you a better lawyer. If you want to give a client a good impression, win the case. Someone has to pay for high rents and expensive furniture, and that usually comes down to the client having to pay high fees. I've seen big law firms that have simply created a huge bureaucracy within the firm. Then you have clients confused by the law and confused by the firm's bureaucracy of attorneys. Small firms don't have that. You deal with either me or one of my partners. It is very casual here, and I feel that is comfortable for us as lawyers and for the clients as well. It is not a pressure atmosphere, and we all take home pretty nice paychecks, based on charging clients reasonable fees.

Each attorney here works on a lot of cases, but I feel an experienced and knowledgeable attorney can handle a high volume of cases expeditiously and give clients the attention they deserve. Like our clients, we are hardworking, down-to-earth, real people you can talk to."

I Am an Associate at a Large Urban Law Firm

"There is a great deal of work and long hours, but the pay is excellent – much better than I think I could do on my own. There are more than 100 lawyers in the firm, so it's a big shop. If I have one complaint, it is that I don't really feel as though I have control over my career. I don't decide which cases I get. Cases – or work on a particular case – are assigned by one of the partners or a very senior associate.

Because this is a general practice, I get all types of cases to work on and I like that. There are times I would like to work on a criminal case or a personal injury case, but you don't make that call, though, in fairness, you can request it and see what happens. Even if I bring a case into the firm, there is no guarantee that I will work on that particular case.

I have been out of law school four years and I've been at the firm three years. This was my first job. The associates talk about becoming partners. Not everyone wants that responsibility, however. An associate is an employee who picks up a paycheck with no management worries. As a partner, you have to try to make the firm better, stronger, and more profitable. You decide the direction the firm should go in. With that responsibility, you have much more say in where your career is going.

There is a lot of office politics – many personalities to deal with. Big law firms have to attract big clients. These clients can be very demanding, and they should be for the money they are paying. Sometimes the partners decide to turn down a case because there just isn't enough profit in it for them.

We do pro bono work, but it often relates to some cause that one of our big clients is involved in. We don't get involved in many cases to help the poor and I'd like to see us do more of that, since we are in an urban area. While I can't say for sure, it is probably just not economically feasible for this firm to represent the indigent.

One advantage of working here is that no expense is spared. If you need something to make your case, like an expert witness, most of our clients have no problem paying for that. I have learned a great deal, but I have not been exposed to every situation; that will take many years. The experienced lawyers here are top-notch. You see the best in action. They really know the tricks of the trade. You pick up legal strategies and techniques you might never encounter working for a smaller firm.

The move up the ladder is rather slow for the amount of work you put in. I am involved in the simpler aspects of cases. I write briefs, do research, attend settlement conferences, and make some court appearances, mostly to handle pretrial motions. The partners and the more experienced senior associates handle a case at the advanced stages, including trials.

I'd like to represent more clients in court. However, I have learned that this job requires patience. I think the partners like to see that you are hungry, eager to get ahead, and want more responsibility. You never really know when or if they are planning to give you that big break, a chance to show what you could do in court or how you would fare playing hardball at a major settlement conference."

PERSONAL QUALIFICATIONS

CREATIVITY MAY NOT BE THE FIRST THING that comes to mind when you think of the personal traits a lawyer must possess, but it is an integral part of the job. Lawyers have to be creative when addressing a jury. They must present a compelling argument during opening and closing statements to get jurors thinking about a case in ways they might not have without the attorney's persuasive presentation. Creativity is important in thinking of innovative ways to settle cases and coming up with win-win solutions. Contracts often have to address complicated issues that can be handled through a novel clause or two written into the agreement by an attorney who was able to think outside the box.

Fine-tuned analytical skills help lawyers make sense out of volumes of information and boil it all down to the bare essentials. They look at the information logically so they can make reasonable judgments about what is at the root of a case and what might be done to bring about a reasonable solution.

Perseverance is a worthwhile talent any good lawyer has to bring to the job. Cases are rarely resolved quickly. If there was an easy solution, the case probably would have been resolved long before lawyers got involved. It often comes down to one side wearing down the other. Tenacity is the key – the ability to see the case through to its successful conclusion.

The work often requires hours of research. To some degree, lawyers have to be detectives, to research every aspect of a case and put a puzzle together without having all the pieces. They search for answers hidden in mounds of precedents. That calls for excellent reading comprehension abilities, with an emphasis on getting through weighty material quickly, understanding it, and figuring out how it affects your case.

Being able to turn a phrase comes in very handy as well. Just ask attorney-turned-best-selling author John Grisham. Writing best sellers aside, the words you write in a motion, brief, or contract can be just as important, and will directly impact the lives of the people involved in a case. The right words are weapons in the legal profession. Reading and writing are not enough. You have to be a passionate speaker as well. It is not just what you say, it is how you say it. Do you believe it? Can you get others to believe it as well? That can make or break a case.

Do you pay attention to every detail? Good lawyers do. Overlook nothing, because the smallest point can change the outcome of a case. Most will miss these buried nuggets of information, and that can set you apart in this field. So can communicating effectively with your client. Do you ask the right questions and listen carefully to the answers? Lawyer-client communication is vital. Equally as important is the way you communicate with others involved in a case. Setting the proper professional tone can help you come out ahead.

It should go without saying that lawyers must have high moral standards. Honesty and integrity are at the heart of this field, along with professionalism and safeguarding your clients' rights and confidentiality. There can be no compromise on these points.

ATTRACTIVE FEATURES

THERE ARE MANY ADVANTAGES TO being a lawyer. Besides the obvious ones of prestige, earnings potential, and mental stimulation and challenge, here are a few you might not have considered.

Depending on the types of cases you handle, you could travel the country representing clients, and if those clients associate with celebrities, entertainers, or sports stars, you as their attorney, might get a chance to do that as well. For instance, if you represent a real estate company that rents out properties to the rich and famous, you would handle all the legal paperwork and meet with all the parties involved. Many times these professional relationships lead to a few invites to glittering social gatherings when all the legal work is completed.

Many lawyers write books, act as consultants for TV shows and movies, and appear as experts on television news programs focusing on legal aspects of issues of the day. Some lecture, teach, or go into politics – both as candidates and as political advisors – all opportunities that come their way because they have a legal background.

Your legal education and all you learn while working as a lawyer will serve you well for the rest of your life, whether you want to remain an attorney your entire professional career or follow another path in your later years. Legal skills are always marketable and you will never be replaced by a computer or outsourced to another country.

The work environment for a lawyer in general practice is very professional, with comfortable offices usually in upscale or modern buildings.

You are not dealing with the same types of cases every day. Sometimes you will be in court; other times you will be occupied with probing research. Writing contracts, wills, briefs, and other legal documents is part of the job, as is interviewing witnesses for a case. You might go out to an accident scene or spend time meeting with the parties to a lawsuit trying to negotiate a settlement.

Lawyers get to be creative. Not every case is uniform. Some cases seem like lost causes from the start, but if you believe in the client, want to have an impact, and are determined to find a way to win the case, you come up with a novel approach, challenge the law, travel the road not usually taken. The sense of satisfaction you get from winning a difficult case is unmatched and it is a wonderful showcase for your legal talents. The tough cases demonstrate just how well you can think under pressure, and you know you went the extra mile for someone.

Since you encounter such a wide variety of cases in a general law practice, it is excellent preparation for a judgeship down the road. What you have been exposed to as a lawyer is always taken into consideration when a politician is thinking of appointing you to a judicial post, or when you are seeking to run for a judgeship or political office.

UNATTRACTIVE ASPECTS

IF YOU DO NOT THRIVE ON TENSION and confrontation, being a lawyer may not be for you. Remember, if you go to court, you are expected to "argue" the case. While attorneys do not fight and dispute all the time, they are known to battle it out with adversaries on a regular basis.

You may clash with other lawyers, clients, witnesses, judges, police officers, even court clerks. You might not flourish in the role of "no more Mr. Nice Guy," but there is no way around that in this field. Working in a calm and serene environment is not in the job description.

Unlike the lawyers on TV, no one wins every case and some losses are tough to take, especially if you believe your client is innocent and getting a raw deal. It is your job to prove your client not guilty or get the court to rule in your client's favor in a civil suit, but sometimes a judge or jury simply does not see things your way and you lose a case you feel you should have won. Those defeats are difficult to deal with and hard to shake off, even though you must. The law is not always fair.

Lawyers often encounter the worst society has to offer. Criminals, scam artists, swindlers, and cheats may be among your clients. Divorces, child custody cases, and family fights over inheritance are always hard to see. So the job can be downright depressing at times, but you have to get past that and focus on the work at hand.

Sometimes a simple suggestion that will settle a matter is summarily dismissed by all sides. Other times one party in a lawsuit is totally unreasonable. You see it all and it can test your faith in humanity, but good lawyers do not let that affect them. They are ready to take the next step and do their best to represent their clients.

There can be a great deal of pressure in this field. Being a lawyer is a high-stress job. Clients and opposing counsel may be on your back constantly. For some of these people, you may never be able to do enough.

Competition abounds in the legal field. If clients do not feel you are doing enough for them, they will fire you no matter how much time and effort you have put into a case.

Whether you have your own law practice or work in a firm, even the most senior attorneys put in long hours and some time on the weekend. That is difficult on you and your family.

The work may be tedious and frustrating. Long hours of research, sometimes failing to yield the precedent you are looking for, may be exasperating and trying on the nerves.

Being a lawyer is a business and some people may balk at paying your bill, no matter how reasonable, and even though they agreed to the fee ahead of time.

EDUCATION AND TRAINING

PEOPLE WITH ALL TYPES OF UNDERGRADUATE degrees go to law school. There is no set course of study for people who want to become lawyers and no such thing as "pre-law." So you are just as likely to meet people in law school with bachelor's degrees in English literature or history as you are to find students with undergraduate degrees in accounting or economics.

In college, take something you like, will do well in, and can fall back on if a legal career does not work out for you. Remember, even if you get into law school, there is no guarantee you will graduate and pass the bar.

Lawyers are analytical, so take a logical approach to going to law school. Law school is time-consuming and expensive. Be absolutely sure you want to be in the legal profession before you embark on this path. Do not go to law school because you believe being a lawyer is a profession where you can make a lot of money. You may be bitterly disappointed, especially if you find that the field is overflowing with people just looking for a big paycheck. This is a career you really have to love.

When considering candidates for admission, law schools take into account a student's grade point average (GPA) and Law School Admission Test (LSAT) scores. There is much more that goes into the process than raw numbers. Law schools like to assemble a varied student body, with people from all walks of life who are not only smart but give the school a distinctive character. For instance, a student who has overcome an obstacle, like a traumatic accident or a serious illness, may be an appealing candidate. A well-written and thoughtful personal statement from a student is an attention grabber.

As you approach your junior year in college, you should start thinking about taking the LSAT. While you would like to do well the first time you take the test, you can take it three times in two years and improve your score. All scores are sent on to the law schools you apply to. Some law schools will consider it a mark against you if you did not do well the first time, but many do not.

Apply to law schools that are likely to accept you. Boston College Law School has a very useful website that can help you gauge which law schools would be the best for you to apply to:

http://www.bc.edu/offices/careers/gradschool/law/research/lawlocator.html

Law schools are located throughout the country, probably more than a few close by. They are grouped by competitive schools, reach schools, and safety schools.

Make sure the law schools you are applying to are accredited by the American Bar Association (ABA). Students who attend schools that are not ABA-accredited may not be eligible to take the bar exam in many states.

Consider tuition and fees. A big-name school with a national reputation may not be for you. You may not like the atmosphere. It might be too high-pressure and may not suit your needs. If you want to be a local attorney, you might want to go to a local law school that has a solid reputation in your area and costs less than a brand-name school.

Law school is what you make of it. Many people think prominent law professors will spoon-feed them the material. Not true. After a while, it will dawn on you that you have to go out and get the information yourself. You become your own teacher. The teaching staff will give you direction, but doing research is mostly up to you. Unlike other educational programs, there is very little handholding in law school.

You do not have to enter law school right after finishing your undergraduate studies. Many people work for a few years before tackling law school. That is not a bad idea and not frowned upon by law schools. Called "nontraditional students," these potential lawyers may attend law school after age thirty. For these candidates, law school admission counselors will consider not only GPA from undergraduate work and LSAT scores, but also work-related experience and community activities. This can often be helpful in getting into law school. The schools feel nontraditional students are more mature, focused, and have greater discipline, and their work experience is seen as a positive, rather than a negative.

Abraham Lincoln, one of the nation's most famous attorneys, never attended law school. He was self-taught and then passed an oral examination to be admitted to the Illinois bar. There is still a way to take the bar exam without attending law school, though that is a very rare occurrence today. Virginia, Vermont, Washington state, and California, allow aspiring lawyers to do on-the-job training and apprenticeships and then take the bar exam. Vermont, for instance, requires an aspiring attorney to study for four years in a law office under the supervision of a licensed attorney with at least three years' experience. The other three states have similar requirements.

No legal education is complete until a person passes the bar exam. The bar exam is a lengthy test to determine if a candidate is qualified to practice law in a particular jurisdiction. The exam has to be taken in the state where you want to practice, so it makes sense to attend a law school in that state. There are courses available to prepare people to take the bar exam, and the test can be taken more than once if you fail.

EARNINGS

HOW MUCH DOES A LAWYER EARN IN a year? Many factors, including the size of your legal practice, the types of cases you are handling, and the clientele you serve, all figure in your compensation as an attorney.

Depending on where in the country you work, you will find a great disparity in earnings. For instance, the highest-paying jobs in the legal field are in Boston, Chicago, New York City, Los Angeles, and Washington. But that does not mean you cannot make money in other locations throughout the nation.

MSNBC recently reported that lawyers are the fifth-highest-paid wage earners in the nation, with an average yearly income of about $130,000. Only physicians, dentists, chief executive officers, and petroleum engineers bring home bigger paychecks than attorneys. If you can snag a job just out of law school at a prestigious law firm, you might earn $160,000, and top the average yearly income as you are just getting started. Most lawyers start at salaries between $90,000 to $125,000 after passing the bar exam – some a bit lower. There is no set standard; it all depends on the firm you work for.

These figures are nationwide averages. In New York City,

for instance, the average yearly income for an attorney is almost $175,000, according to US News & World Report. In San Francisco, a lawyer's average annual salary is about $170,000; Salt Lake City, $125,000; and the state of Alaska, $100,000.

There is no ceiling on attorneys' earnings. Top lawyers anywhere in the country can easily make over a half million dollars a year or more.

Lawyers usually charge by the hour. Very often they get a retainer in advance, and charge the hourly rate against the retainer. Lawyers can always work on a contingency basis when lawsuits involve winning monetary damages, as in a personal injury case. Most law firms offer benefits, including health insurance, and some firms also have retirement plans.

OPPORTUNITIES

THERE ARE MANY LAWYERS IN THE United States. The American Bar Association estimates that 1.3 million are currently in practice. Even though lawyers abound, many are needed, and not simply to handle high-priced or high-profile cases. Middle-class people and the working poor need lawyers and can afford to pay a fee, but not an exorbitant one. This constitutes a growth opportunity in the field.

Lawyers in private general practice can make a good living by looking at their practice as a volume business. They can build a large clientele, all paying a fee they can afford. You are helping a segment of the population that needs legal assistance and often hesitates to seek it out because they feel they cannot afford it. Help a few people at a reasonable fee and they will recommend you to others. Word will start getting around and you can build a nice practice with a steady income. It is about developing a solid client base, especially for young attorneys looking to strike out on their own and get a practice going.

Traditionally, general practice attorneys addressed clients' legal issues from "womb to tomb," meaning the attorney handled people's legal matters throughout their entire lifetime, and often did that for everyone in the family. That was very appealing to clients because the lawyer was someone they knew and trusted for years, someone who knew their family, and someone who could tackle a variety of problems. That is an area of law that is growing today. In the impersonal digital world, more and more people want to be able to turn to someone they know, have confidence in, and can talk to face-to-face about everyday legal matters, like wills and estates, closings, tax issues, business matters, contracts, tenant-landlord disputes, municipal court appearances, and a host of other law-related problems. In an age of specialization, there is still a need for general practice attorneys.

Many lawyers gravitate to heavily populated urban areas because that is where the people are, but potential clients are found in sparsely populated areas as well. As with any business, you have to find an area where your services are needed. Do not underestimate how many people need legal services.

Some nonprofit, community-based organizations get either government funds or grants to aid poor people in need of legal services. These agencies will pay your fee and you can help these individuals with a variety of legal problems. Look around you, at people you know. Legal problems are everywhere. Ask yourself, how can I be of service?

GETTING STARTED

IT MIGHT TAKE YEARS FOR YOU TO LAND a job in that prestigious downtown law firm you have been eyeing ever since you thought about becoming a lawyer. So why wait? You are a lawyer. You just spent years in school and countless hours studying for the bar exam. You need some practical legal experience, a chance to see what is out there, so get some cases under your belt. They can come from friends, relatives, or by spending time at a legal clinic aiding people who need legal services. Young lawyers have to get out in the legal community. You need to get your name around, meet people in the field, start making contacts and networking, and see what you can do. As with any business, experience is important in the legal field and you do not acquire it by sitting around waiting for a job offer. Sole practitioners in your area might be struggling with an abundance of work and just might need a young lawyer to help them with the overflow. That might even lead to a job.

Some lawyers just starting out share office space. They do not form a law firm or partnership. They are simply sharing the cost of the rent, clerical help, and other business expenses. They have their own clients and none of the obligations of a law firm or partnership.

Many communities have incubators – small, usually inexpensive, office space in a large office building that is shared by various businesspeople in a variety of fields.

Geared toward start-ups, these incubators give you everything you need to have a place of your own to conduct business and start a general law practice. Alternatively, you can always work out of your home and save a few dollars on rent.

Does starting your own law practice sound like a lot of work? It is. You may have to put in 50- or 60-plus hours a week to get it up and running. That is just about the same amount of time the partners at that big downtown law firm would expect you to put in when you started working there. New lawyers just out of law school, who land jobs at big law firms, start at the bottom rung. That means they put in long hours each week. You may be on the fast track, but it can be a long slog. Law school is hard work but it is merely a prelude to what the job is all about.

There are benefits to being on your own. One of them is that you can choose your own clients. You might not like some of the clients at that big law firm, but you have no say in whether or not to handle their cases. Of course, the firm pays your business expenses and gives you a paycheck each week, though it might be a bit lower than you expected. The law is no different than any other business – it might take you a while to earn what you feel you are worth.

ASSOCIATIONS

■ **American Bar Association (ABA)**
http://www.americanbar.org/aba.html

■ **National Bar Association**
http://www.nationalbar.org

■ **National Lawyers Association (NLA)**
http://www.nla.org

■ **National Lawyers Guild (NLG)**
https://www.nlg.org

■ **Hispanic National Bar Association (HNBA)**
http://hnba.com

■ **National Association of Women Lawyers (NAWL)**
http://www.nawl.org

■ **The National Trial Lawyers**
http://www.thenationaltriallawyers.org

■ **National Association of Minority & Women Owned Law Firms (NAMWOLF)**
http://www.namwolf.org

■ **Black Women Lawyers Association (BWLA)**
http://www.bwla.org

■ **National Academy of Elder Law Attorneys (NAELA)**
https://www.naela.org

PERIODICALS

The National Law Journal
The American Lawyer
USLAW Magazine
Attorney At Law Magazine
Lawyer & Statesman
The National Jurist
ABA Journal
New Jersey Law Journal
New York Law Journal
Texas Lawyer
Delaware Law Weekly
The Legal Intelligencer
Student Lawyer

WEBSITES

■ **LawyerEdu.org**
http://www.lawyeredu.org

■ **LAW.COM**
http://www.law.com

■ **Boston College On-line Law School Locator**
www.bc.edu/offices/careers/gradschool/law
/research/lawlocator.html

■ **National Association for Law Placement (NALP)**
http://www.nalp.org

■ **American Association for Justice**
https://www.justice.org

■ **American Law Institute (ALI)**
https://www.ali.org

■ **Association for Continuing Legal Education (ACLEA)**
http://www.aclea.org

■ **Defense Research Institute (DRI)**
http://www.dri.org

■ **The National Black Lawyers-Top 100**
http://www.nbltop100.org

■ **HG.org Legal Resources**
www.hg.org/northam-bar.html

■ **FindLaw.com**
http://stu.findlaw.com/index.html

■ **Southern Poverty Law Center (SPLC)**
http://www.splcenter.org

■ **Association of American Law Schools (AALS)**
http://www.aals.org

■ **Notes: Each state has its own bar association. For a list go to www.hg.org/northam-bar.htm**

■ **Many law schools throughout the country publish their own law journals. A list of law school websites can be found at http://stu.findlaw.com/schools/fulllist.html**